STEP-UP
HISTORY

Famous Irish Men and Women

Sean Sheehan

Evans

Published by Evans Brothers Limited
2A Portman Mansions
Chiltern Street
London W1U 6NR

© Evans Brothers Limited 2008

Produced for Evans Brothers Limited by
White-Thomson Publishing Ltd,
Bridgewater Business Centre,
210 High Street,
Lewes, East Sussex BN7 2NH

Printed in Hong Kong by New Era Printing Co. Ltd.

Project manager: Sonya Newland

Designer: Robert Walster

Consultant: Brian Malone

British Library Cataloguing in Publication Data

Sheehan, Sean
Famous Irish men and women. - (Step up history)

  Famous Irish men and women. - (Step up
  history)
  1. Celebrities - Ireland - Biography - Juvenile
  literature
  2. Ireland - Biography - Juvenile literature

I. Title
920'.0415

ISBN-13: 9780237534325

Picture acknowledgements:

akg-images: page 19 (Green Film Company);
Alamy: page 15 (Stephen Saks Photography);
Corbis: pages 1 (Reuters), 7 (Bettmann), 8 (The
Irish Image College), 10 (Bettmann), 11 (Alain le
Garsmeuer), 12 (Richard T. Nowitz), 13 (Bettmann),
14 and cover top right (Sean Sexton Collection), 16
(Steffan Schmidt/epa), 17l (Lorenzo Ciniglio), 20
(Henri Bureau/Sygma), 21 and cover (Paul
Faith/Pool/epa), 22 (Reuters), 23 (Benedicte
Kurzen/epa), 24 and cover top left (Reuters), 25
(Afolabo Sotunde/Reuters); Getty Images: pages 18
(General Photographic Agency), 27 (John Peters);
Popperfoto: page 26; Topfoto.co.uk: pages 9 (The
British Library/HIP), 17r (Topham).

Illustrative work by Robert Walster.

Contents

Introduction

In this book you will find out about 14 famous Irish people. All of them, in their different ways, deserve to be famous. They come from different times in history and have very different backgrounds. For example, Brian Bórú became ruler of all Ireland in the eleventh century and Grace O'Malley ruled part of the country in the sixteenth century, but Michael Collins was a farmer's son and James Connolly grew up in Scotland in extreme poverty.

Changing times

As you learn about the lives and achievements of these people, try to think about changes that have taken place through time. For example, in transport, what differences would there be between the way that Brian Bórú travelled to Dublin and the way that Michael Collins travelled? What weapons might each of them have used in their wars? What might Grace O'Malley have to say to Sonia O'Sullivan after watching her race? After you have read about the four women included here, you could write a play in which they talk to each other about their lives and how different they are.

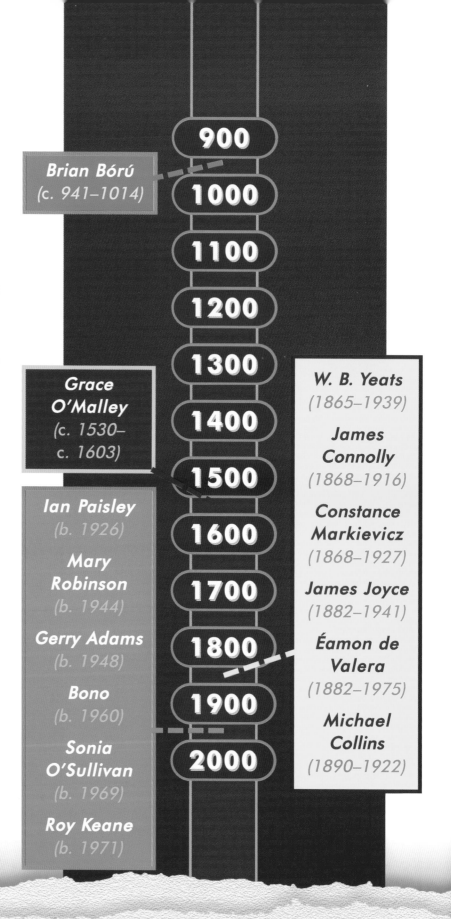

900

Brian Bórú
(c. 941–1014)

1000

1100

1200

1300

Grace
O'Malley
(c. 1530–
c. 1603)

1400

W. B. Yeats
(1865–1939)

James
Connolly
(1868–1916)

1500

Constance
Markievicz
(1868–1927)

Ian Paisley
(b. 1926)

1600

Mary
Robinson
(b. 1944)

1700

James Joyce
(1882–1941)

Gerry Adams
(b. 1948)

1800

Éamon de
Valera
(1882–1975)

Bono
(b. 1960)

1900

Michael
Collins
(1890–1922)

Sonia
O'Sullivan
(b. 1969)

2000

Roy Keane
(b. 1971)

Beyond Ireland

Most of these people were born and lived in Ireland for most of their lives, but millions more Irish people emigrated to other countries and many of them became famous in their new homes. What do you think makes a person Irish? Is James Connolly Irish if he was born in Scotland and is Sonia O'Sullivan Irish if she has recently become an Australian citizen?

▶ *This map shows the places in Ireland that are mentioned in this book. Perhaps you could make a class display with biographies of famous people linked to places on a map.*

Belfast

Innisfree

CONNACHT

Galway

Tara

Clontarf

Dublin

LEINSTER

Limerick

MUNSTER

Cork

Cobh

Brian Bórú (c. 941–1014)

In Brian Bórú's time Ireland was divided into many small kingdoms. Each had its own ruler. Brian's father was one of these rulers.

The Vikings

For 200 years Vikings had been settling in Ireland. They often married Irish people and learned to speak Gaelic, but they also attacked neighbouring towns to take slaves and valuables. Brian's mother was killed in a Viking raid when he was a young boy. Limerick was a Viking town near where he lived, and Brian probably took part in raids against the Vikings in his youth.

King of Munster

In AD 951 Brian's older brother Mathgamain became king. He fought many battles to increase his lands and wealth. He always ended battles by making peace with his enemies. After one successful battle in 976 Mathgamain was murdered while discussing peace with the king he had beaten.

▶ Brian Bórú's rule spread outwards from Limerick, as he defeated other Irish leaders.

Brian became king and took revenge on the people who had killed his brother. His kingdom grew bigger until he ruled all of Munster. He became a skilled leader and built up a navy as well as an army. He used ships to attack towns along the coasts and along the River Shannon, the longest river in Ireland.

Tara

Clontarf
• 1014

Dublin

Limerick

MUNSTER

High King of Ireland

Eventually Brian won control of most of Ireland, and in 999 he fought a great battle against Sitric Silkenbeard, the Viking ruler of Dublin. The armies fought for an entire day and Brian was victorious. He was named High King of Ireland. His rule lasted for 15 more years until, in 1014, another fierce battle was fought between Brian's armies and those of rebel leaders from Leinster at Clontarf. Brian's forces won the battle, but Brian was killed.

Brian is remembered as the first king to unite the whole country under one ruler. Besides fighting many battles he also gave money to churches to rebuild the damage caused by Viking raids and helped replace their stolen libraries of ancient manuscripts.

▲ *This engraving shows Brian Bórú being attacked by a Viking during the Battle of Clontarf in 1014.*

How do we know about Brian Bórú?

Several ancient manuscripts tell the story of Brian Bórú. One of them, *The War of the Irish with Foreigners*, was commissioned by Brian's great-grandson, Muirchertach. Why do you think Brian's great-grandson would commission this story? How might the story have been affected by the fact that one of Brian's descendants was paying for it to be written?

Grace O'Malley (c. 1530–c. 1603)

Grace O'Malley, also known as Granuaile, was born around 1530. She was the daughter of one of the powerful chiefs of Connacht. She married Donal O'Flaherty, the son of a neighbouring chief, when she was 16, and they had three children. Unusually for women of that time, Grace O'Malley managed her family's business and this involved trade with France, Spain and Portugal.

▲ *Rockfleet Castle was Grace's home after she married Richard Bourke. From here she reigned as a pirate queen. The tower house was restored in the twentieth century by a direct descendant of Grace.*

The English arrive

During Grace's lifetime, English forces were gaining more control over Ireland. Many Irish chiefs were forced to submit to foreign rule, but Grace remained independent. She had her own small fleet of trading ships and used some of them as pirate ships. With her own force of men, Grace attacked and robbed ships belonging to the Irish chiefs who had submitted to the English.

A pirate queen

In 1566, after her first husband had died, Grace married another local chief. His name was Richard Bourke and Grace moved to live with him in Rockfleet Castle, on the coast of Connacht. Her reputation as a pirate grew so fearsome that local merchants called on the English to control her activities. The English tried to catch Grace and stop her from attacking the Irish chiefs.

In 1577, Grace was finally captured and imprisoned by the English. She managed to negotiate her release in 1579, and as soon as she was free she went back to being a pirate queen. In 1593, after the death of Richard Bourke, she travelled to London with some other local chiefs to complain about English rule in her part of Ireland. She met with Queen Elizabeth I and asked to

Write an article

There are many colourful legends about Grace O'Malley, especially about her life in Connacht. The website below has links to lots of other sites telling Grace's story. Pick your favourite event in her life and then write a newspaper article that might have appeared at the time, talking about the event. Remember to include a dramatic headline, and find a picture to use with your article.

■ http://www.omalley-clan.org/uow/
omalley_web/granuaile_history.htm

be allowed to own the land that had belonged to her second husband. This was not allowed under Gaelic law but Grace wanted to remain an independent woman. She was successful and returned to Ireland. Grace died around 1603 and is still remembered as a famous Irish ruler.

◀ *Grace O'Malley meets Queen Elizabeth I. The queen granted Grace ownership of the lands that had belonged to her second husband in Ireland.*

W. B. Yeats (1865–1939)

The poet and playwright William Butler Yeats was born into a wealthy landowning family in Ireland. He grew up in the Irish countryside but was educated in London and then Dublin. He began writing poetry while he was still at school. There he became interested in Irish mythology and folk stories, which he used in his poetry. When he was a young man he became very attracted to a woman named Maude Gonne. She was an Irish Nationalist and he proposed marriage to her many times throughout his life. Maude did not want to marry him, but they remained close friends. She encouraged Yeats to take an interest in Irish politics.

The Irish Literary Revival

The Irish Literary Revival movement, led by Yeats and the very rich Lady Gregory, encouraged Irish writers and translated old Irish folk tales into English. Yeats and Lady Gregory created the Abbey Theatre in Dublin and put on plays by Irish playwrights. They also published novels and poetry by Irish people who might never have had their work published otherwise.

▲ W. B. Yeats, with the artist Lady Lavery, at a garden party in 1925. This picture was taken while Yeats was a senator.

The Irish Free State

Yeats's early poetry and plays were based on Irish folk stories, but he also began to pay attention to the struggle for Irish independence that was taking place in the early part of the twentieth century. Some of his more famous poems, such as 'Easter 1916', are about the struggle for independence.

In 1921 part of Ireland – the 26 counties in the south – became independent, while six counties in the north remained part of Britain. In 1922 Yeats became a member of the Irish senate, the part of the Irish parliament that decides on new laws. His most famous debate was over the issue of divorce. Irish Catholic leaders were against divorce, although it was permitted in Britain. Yeats warned the other senators that if they made divorce impossible in Ireland, it would mean the 26 counties could never be reunited with the other six counties.

▶ *On Yeats's headstone, in Drumcliff cemetery, are carved the words 'Cast a cold Eye, On life, on Death. Horseman, pass by!' These are taken from his poem 'Under Ben Bulben'.*

'The Lake Isle of Innisfree'

These are the opening lines of one of Yeats' most famous poems:

I will arise and go now and go to Innisfree,
And a small cabin build there,
  of clay and wattles made:
Nine bean rows will I have there,
  a hive for the honey bee;
And live alone in the bee-loud glade.

Draw a picture of Innisfree as Yeats describes it. How does Yeats feel about this place? Why do you think he feels this way?

Later years

In 1923 Yeats was awarded the Nobel Prize for Literature and became very famous. He was the first Irish person to be awarded this prize. He also became interested in the occult and took part in séances.

As he grew older, he travelled in Europe and became less interested in Irish politics. He continued to write, though, and is remembered as one of the most important poets to write in the English language.

On headstone:
Cast a cold Eye
On Life, on Death.
Horseman, pass by!

W. B. YEATS

June 13th 1865
January 28th 1939

James Connolly (1868–1916)

James Connolly was born in Edinburgh to poor Irish immigrant parents. At the age of 14 he joined the British army and spent seven years as a soldier in Ireland. While he was there, Irish people were fighting to be independent from Britain and to stop paying rents to British landlords. British soldiers were often sent to deal with demonstrations and to arrest the leaders of the Irish Nationalists.

Struggling to survive

In 1888 Connolly left the army and returned to Scotland, where he read all he could about socialism – the belief that things should be shared out among everyone rather than being owned by individuals. He began to write and give lectures about these beliefs. Soon people started to think he was something of a troublemaker and no one would employ him.

In 1896 Connolly moved to Dublin to organise the Dublin Socialist Club. The pay was not enough to support his family so he also worked as a labourer. Life was very difficult and in 1903 he emigrated to America. His family joined him there after he had found work.

The 1913 Lock-Out

By 1910, however, Connolly was back in Ireland and organising trade unions. Poor people in Dublin lived in terrible conditions and most people who had jobs worked long hours. In 1913 around 20,000 men went on strike to demand better conditions. The employers refused to let them back to work and a few months later the strike failed, as starving people were forced to accept the employers' rules.

James Connolly is remembered as a great leader in the Irish fight for independence. This statue of him stands in Dublin.

The Easter Rising

James Connolly is best known for his part in the Easter Rising. At Easter 1916, armed Irish Nationalists seized part of the city of Dublin. Connolly was the leader of the rebels and his troops took over the General Post Office (GPO). The rebels declared an Irish state and Connolly was made deputy president. They held out under attack in the GPO for five days.

The Easter Rising failed, though. When the rebels surrendered, most of the main street in Dublin had been destroyed and many Nationalists had been killed. Connolly was arrested, and although he was seriously wounded and probably dying, he was condemned to death and shot by firing squad.

Easter Rising timeline

Using the website below and other Internet resources, find out more about the Easter Rising of 1916 and James Connolly's involvement in it. Draw a timeline of events leading up to Connolly's death. Illustrate it with pictures of the people involved and the events that took place.

■ http://www.bbc.co.uk/history/british/easterrising/

▼ *This photograph, taken in April 1916, shows Sackville Street in Dublin after the Easter Rising. Many of the buildings have been destroyed by the fighting.*

Constance Markievicz (1868–1927)

This portrait of Constance Markiewicz demonstrates her wealth and status. She did not take up her position in parliament because her party did not acknowledge government from London.

Constance Markievicz was born into a rich Anglo-Irish family. They owned a large house in Ireland, had many servants, and lived a life of luxury. Constance travelled around Europe and went to art school in London.

In 1899, Constance met a Russian count and the two fell in love. They enjoyed a lively social life, but Constance started to take an interest in the Irish Nationalist movement. She knew the Nationalist leader James Connolly and began to support his cause. She also started to give money to poor Dublin families.

A letter of explanation

Constance Markievicz might have led a life of wealth and pleasure. Instead she became involved in the struggle for Irish independence, spent her entire fortune helping poor Irish people and took part in a war. Imagine you are Constance in prison in England. Write a letter to your family, explaining why you chose this path. What are your feelings about Irish independence and the plight of the ordinary Irish people?

The Citizen's Army

Constance was involved in the 1913 Lock-Out. Once she was caught in a riot and beaten by a policeman. She began to run soup kitchens for the families of the strikers. In 1914, after the strike had failed, Constance joined the Citizen's Army. She became a captain and trained with her men at weekends. During the Easter Rising, Constance and the Citizen's Army took over a square in the centre of Dublin – St Stephen's Green. When the rebels surrendered she was arrested and condemned to death. Just before she was due to be executed, however, she was reprieved and sent to prison in England.

▶ A memorial to Constance Markievicz in St Stephen's Green, Dublin. Constance was in the Irish Citizen's Army that fought for rights for Irish workers.

CONSTANCE
MARKIEVICZ

MAJOR
IRISH CITIZEN ARMY
1916

Irish independence

In 1918 Constance became the first woman ever to be elected to the British House of Commons. She then returned to Ireland, where she became a leader in the rebel government. In 1919 war broke out between groups of Nationalists and the British government. Constance remained in Dublin, travelling around the city in disguise, attending Nationalist meetings.

In 1921 the war ended with a peace treaty that gave independence to 26 counties of Ireland. Constance opposed the treaty because six counties in the north of Ireland remained part of Britain. Civil war broke out in Ireland and at the end of it the treaty and partition was accepted. Although most of Ireland now had its own government, people still went hungry and there were not enough jobs to go around. Constance continued to use her own money to help the Irish poor.

Constance died of appendicitis in 1927. Thousands of people attended her funeral.

James Joyce (1882–1941)

Ireland has many famous writers, but James Joyce is one of the best-known. He is now highly respected in Ireland, but this was not always the case. When Joyce was alive, he did not like Irish society and felt that people did not appreciate his writing.

Joyce first left Ireland when he was 20. He made a few short return visits but the rest of his life was spent in various European cities. When he died in Switzerland in 1941, few people in Ireland paid any attention to his death. It was only many years later that he came to be recognised as one of Ireland's greatest writers.

▶ *This statue of James Joyce sits beside his grave in Switzerland. Joyce was better-known in Europe than he was in his native Ireland.*

A Dublin childhood

James Joyce did not come from a poor family, but his father did not manage his money well. In the 20 years he spent in Dublin, James and his family moved house 14 times. This was often because they could not afford to pay the rent.

James was mostly educated in Jesuit schools, and was encouraged to become a priest. However, as he grew older he turned away from his religion and stopped believing in God. He became increasingly interested in literature and started to write poetry.

On 16 June 1904 James went for a walk with Nora Barnacle, a woman he had met a few days earlier. Nora was from Galway and was working as a chambermaid in a Dublin hotel. James and Nora left Ireland in October of that year. They remained together until James died 37 years later, although they were only married in 1931.

Fame in Europe

Living in Europe, James Joyce gradually became known as a very special writer. He wrote poetry, plays and short stories. His novel *Ulysses* – which made him very famous – imagined a day in the life of a Dublin man. The man he imagined was called Leopold Bloom and the day in his life was 16 June 1904. James Joyce spent 17 years writing his next novel, *Finnegan's Wake*, and he died shortly after it was completed.

Bloomsday

Use the Internet and other resources to find out more about Bloomsday.

■ How is Bloomsday celebrated in Dublin?

■ Where else is it celebrated and how?

■ Why do you think James Joyce chose 16 June as the day to write about in *Ulysses*?

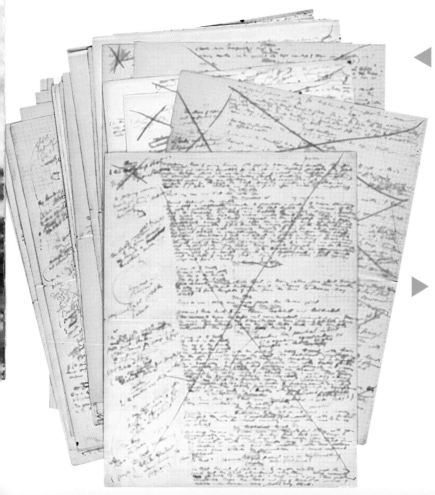

◀ *James Joyce wrote obsessively. He would write and rewrite, scoring out large passages until he was completely happy with the result. These pages are from his famous novel* Ulysses.

▶ *People celebrating Bloomsday outside the Joyce Centre in Dublin. On Bloomsday, people dress up in Edwardian clothes and walk through the streets, just as the hero of* Ulysses *did.*

Éamon de Valera (1882–1975)

During one of the most important periods of Irish history – as the country moved towards independence – two men were fighting to win freedom from Britain. Éamon de Valera and Michael Collins first worked together for Ireland's freedom, but during the Irish Civil War they found themselves on opposite sides.

Éamon de Valera was one of the leaders of the 1916 Easter Rising and the later war against Britain. In 1921, when the British were ready to give independence to Ireland, Michael Collins negotiated the settlement. De Valera refused to accept the agreement and a civil war broke out between those who supported the treaty, led by Michael Collins, and those who opposed it. De Valera's side lost the war but he refused to accept the new government until 1927. After elections in 1932, his party won and he became the head of the Irish government. He was taoiseach several times and in 1959 he became president of Ireland.

▶ *Éamon de Valera giving a speech in America around 1919. He went to the United States to campaign for funds, and it was here that he was declared to be president of the Irish Republic.*

De Valera's contribution

People in Ireland tend to either support de Valera or strongly dislike him. He has been criticised because, it is claimed, he could have stopped the civil war in 1921. De Valera's supporters refer to the Irish constitution, which he created. They point out how important this was and how it has hardly been altered since it was adopted in 1937.

Michael Collins (1890–1922)

Michael Collins also fought in the Easter Rising and went to prison. In the war against Britain he was a great military leader, organising his men into guerrilla groups, which made it difficult for the British to defeat them.

▶ *This is a still from the film Michael Collins (1996). It shows Collins, played by Liam Neeson, rallying support for Irish independence.*

Looking back at the civil war

Éamon de Valera lived for a long time after the troubled period of the 1920s, while Michael Collins died still fighting for his country. If both of them had lived until their old age what do you think they might have said to each other after they had retired? Write a play in which the two elderly men talk about what happened, and act this out with a friend.

The Anglo-Irish Treaty

In 1921 Collins negotiated the peace treaty with Britain, believing that he could persuade de Valera and others to accept it. When de Valera and his supporters refused to accept the terms of the treaty, Collins tried hard to prevent the civil war. He failed, though, and eventually led the war against de Valera's side, all the time trying to persuade them to stop fighting. He was assassinated by anti-Treaty forces in 1922. He was given a state funeral.

Ian Paisley (b. 1926)

Since the division of Ireland into the Republic of Ireland and Northern Ireland in 1921, there has been violent disagreement between people who want to remain part of Britain, the Unionists, and people who want to be reunited with the republic, the Nationalists. From the 1970s two leaders, Gerry Adams and Ian Paisley, led the opposing sides. In 2007 they agreed to share the task of peacefully governing Northern Ireland.

Ian Paisley was an Evangelist minister for many years. He believed that another form of Christianity – Roman Catholicism – was evil and harmful. Over the years he opposed all the attempts to find a peaceful settlement between the Nationalists and Unionists. He became an MP in the British parliament in 1970.

Over the years, Ian Paisley has been criticised for preventing a peaceful settlement by refusing to accept the position of Nationalists. In a speech in 2006 he said:

'Sinn Féin [the Nationalist party] are not fit to be in partnership with decent people. They are not fit to be in the government of Northern Ireland and it will be over our dead bodies if they ever get there.'

Violent times

In the 1970s the violence between Unionists and Nationalists grew much worse. There were murders and bomb attacks in Northern Ireland and England. In 1998 the Belfast Agreement ended the violence, but Paisley opposed this agreement. It was not until 2006 that he accepted the sharing of power in Northern Ireland. He retired as First Minister of the Northern Ireland Assembly in 2008.

◄ *The results of riots in Belfast, Northern Ireland, in 1981 – a burnt-out bus stands in the street.*

Gerry Adams (b. 1948)

Gerry Adams grew up in Belfast in a strongly Nationalist family. He became involved in the Catholic civil rights movement of the 1970s. At that time many Catholics were prevented from voting in local elections. Things became violent and the Nationalists believed that the British army was supporting the Unionists. Illegal armies, such as the IRA and the UDA, started shooting their opponents and planting bombs.

Sinn Féin leader

Gerry Adams became the leader of Sinn Féin, the Nationalist organisation. He went to prison for a time and was elected as an MP, although he refused to take his place in the British parliament. In 1984 he was shot by members of a Loyalist group, but he survived. In 1988 he had become so notorious that the British government banned his voice from television and radio. Actors had to speak the words for him.

In 1988 he began secret talks aimed at bringing about an end to violence in Northern Ireland. In 1994 the IRA called a ceasefire. In 1998 Gerry Adams led the Nationalist negotiations when all parties agreed on a peace settlement. In 2006 the two sides agreed on joint government.

Communities at war

Can you think of any other countries where two communities have been at war with one another in the past? Write a list of the countries you can think of and the solutions they reached to end the internal disagreements.

▲ Ian Paisley (left) and Gerry Adams (right) in the Irish government building in Stormont in March 2007, after they had settled on an historic power-sharing agreement.

Mary Robinson (b. 1944)

Mary Robinson was the first woman to hold the office of president of Ireland and the first woman to be United Nations Commissioner for Human Rights. She has received many awards for her work in human rights.

An early start

Mary went to Trinity College in Dublin and then to Harvard University in the United States to study law. She became a professor of law at Trinity when she was 25 and became a senator in 1969 – a job she held for 20 years. While she was a senator she wanted to change some of the laws of Ireland, including trying to bring in a law that would allow Irish people to get divorced.

President of Ireland

The president of Ireland had always been a figurehead – someone who represented the country but did not actually play a big part in running it. Usually the president was an elderly person. When Mary Robinson decided to become president it was the first time that anyone had challenged who the government had really wanted to do the job. An election was held for the first time – and Mary won.

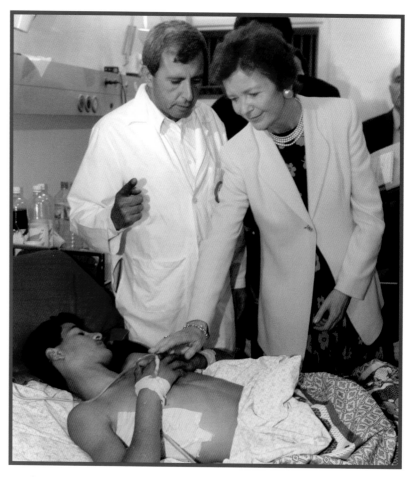

▲ Mary Robinson visits a hospital in the Gaza Strip in her role as United Nations Commissioner for Human Rights in 2000.

Mary made the job an important one. She met international leaders and travelled to countries where there was famine or war in order to publicise their problems. She remained president for seven years and was very popular in Ireland.

The troubles of the world

In 1997 Mary resigned as president in order to take up a position as United Nations Commissioner for Human Rights. As commissioner Mary became very unpopular with world leaders. She criticised a number of countries because of the way that women and prisoners were treated. She also did not like the way some countries dealt with war and other crises. She criticised the United States for its policy of capital punishment. She ended her job as commissioner in 2002 and has recently joined an organisation called the Elders.

The Elders

The Elders are a group led by former president of South Africa Nelson Mandela. The group tries to help countries and people who have problems such as famine or a bad government. Using the website below, find out a bit more about the Elders. Write a brief summary of the key people in the group. What do these people have in common? If you were one of the Elders, which of the world's problems would you deal with first?

■ http://www.theelders.org/

▲ Some of the Elders meet to celebrate Nelson Mandela's birthday in 2007. Mary Robinson is third from left. Can you find out who the other members of the Elders are in this picture?

Bono (b. 1960)

Paul Hewson, given the nickname Bono by a school friend, is the lead singer of Ireland's most successful rock band. U2 was formed by four school friends and they began making records in 1979. At first they were only moderately successful, but then they released two albums – *War* (1983) and *Under a Blood Red Sky* (1983), which made them famous all over the world. Throughout the 1980s and 1990s the band had many hit albums. In 2005 they took their place in the Rock and Roll Hall of Fame. They have won more than 20 awards.

Personal career

Besides singing with U2, Bono has worked on songs and albums with many other musicians and singers, including Frank Sinatra, Johnny Cash, Luciano Pavarotti, Bruce Springsteen, Roy Orbison and Tina Turner. He has a number of other business interests besides music and has become very rich.

▲ Bono on stage during U2's 2005 Vertigo tour. The band is one of the most popular in the world. This concert was in Brussels, Belgium.

Charity work

Since 1979 Bono has helped with many charities. He took part in concerts for Amnesty International, Band Aid and Live Aid as well as Live 8. Since 2000 he has been involved in many charities aimed at helping to prevent the spread of AIDS in Africa.

Bono and others have worked for campaigns such as Drop the Debt. This campaign asked countries like the United States and Britain to cancel debts owed to them by African countries. If poor countries did not have to spend their money on paying interest on loans, people argue, they would have enough to provide doctors and medicine for their citizens. Other people say that cancelling debt is just another form of charity. Some say that charity will only keep a country weak and dependent. What do you think?

▶ *Bono is pictured here with British prime minister Gordon Brown (left) in Nigeria, Africa. The singer travels widely as part of his anti-poverty charity campaigns.*

Celebrity causes

Many pop stars are now involved in political or charity work. Look at the links from the website below and find out which other stars are as active as Bono and the causes they support. Which do you think are the best causes? Why do you think certain celebrities support particular charities? Organise a classroom debate in which different groups argue for certain causes.

■ http://www.ecorazzi.com/

Sonia O'Sullivan (b. 1969)

Sonia O'Sullivan was one of the most successful athletes in her field. She was a middle-distance runner, competing in 5,000 metres, 3,000 metres and 1,500 metres races. She took part in world competitions from 1988 to her retirement in 2007. That is almost 30 years and in that time she won many gold and silver medals in world and European championships, as well as competing in four Olympic Games.

O'Sullivan was born in County Cork, and began running when she was at secondary school. She then won a scholarship to study and train at Pennsylvania's Villanova University in 1987. She trained as a cross-country runner and raced as part of the college's running team.

Back in Ireland, throughout the 1990s she dominated the sport and has a long list of gold medals and national and international speed records. In recent years she has competed in several marathons. She placed well in all of them. She recently became an Australian citizen so that she could compete in some events for Australia. In between the four Olympic Games, Sonia has also made time for her two daughters.

▲ *Sonia O'Sullivan leads the field in the Women's 5,000-metres race at the World Championships in Paris in August 2003.*

Roy Keane (b. 1971)

Roy Keane is one of the most talented football players of modern times. He played professionally for 15 years and is currently manager of the Premier League club Sunderland United.

Born in Cork, Roy played football from an early age and found employment with a local football club called Cobh Wanderers. In 1990 he signed a contract with Nottingham Forest, where he played for two years. In 1992 he transferred to Manchester United. The best years of his career were as Manchester United's captain. He led them to many successes in football, but his years there were also marked by some serious injuries. He became famous for his determination to win and his ability to inspire his team. As captain he was also very outspoken, criticising other team members if he thought they could do better.

Roy played for Ireland many times and caused a great upset in Ireland when he quarrelled with the Irish manager in the World Cup in Korea in 2002. Keane was sent home and the Irish team was knocked out of the competition. Irish people were divided over who was to blame – Roy Keane or the Irish manager, Mick McCarthy.

▲ Roy Keane watches from the touchline as the team he manages, Sunderland, plays the team he once played for – Manchester United.

Glossary

Anglo-Irish   a social class in Ireland made up of people with British ancestry.

assassinated   murdered for political reasons.

capital punishment   the death penalty.

chambermaid   a woman who tidies and cleans the bedrooms in a hotel.

Citizen's Army   an army of about 350 members of the Transport and General Workers Union, set up in 1913 to protect strikers against the police.

civil rights   the rights of a person to freedom of speech, freedom from wrongful arrest, freedom to be given a fair trial, freedom to marry, the right to vote in elections, freedom against discrimination on the grounds of race or religion, etc.

Connacht   an area in the west of Ireland that includes counties Galway, Sligo, Leitrim, Mayo and Roscommon.

constitution   the basic laws of a country.

crises   times of great danger or difficulty.

Easter Rising   the name given to the uprising of Easter 1916, when Nationalist revolutionaries took over parts of Dublin in an attempt to bring about Irish independence.

Evangelist   someone who believes in certain Protestant religious views, including the conversion of the world to their form of Christianity.

figurehead   a person who is at the head of a country or organisation, but whose job is merely to represent rather than lead.

firing squad   a group of soldiers ordered to carry out an execution by shooting.

Gaelic   the original language of Ireland.

Gaelic law   the laws of Ireland before the Norman invasion.

guerrilla   a small group of fighters who hide from their larger enemy and make sudden attacks and then withdraw.

immigrant   someone who has recently arrived in a new country to live.

IRA   Irish Republican Army – a military group dedicated to a reunion of the six counties of Northern Ireland with the 26 counties of the Republic of Ireland.

Jesuits   a Catholic religious group of men who are renowned for running schools and colleges.

landlords   people who own buildings and rent them out to people to live in.

Literary Revival   an Irish movement in the early twentieth century that encouraged Irish writers.

Loyalists   people in Northern Ireland who claim to be loyal to Britain.

manuscripts	handwritten books.
Munster	an area in the south of Ireland that includes counties Cork, Clare, Kerry, Limerick, Tipperary and Waterford.
mythology	a traditional story that is often about magic or the supernatural.
Nationalists	people who want self-government for their country.
Nobel Prize	a series of international prizes given out each year for the best writer, the person who has done the most for peace, the best scientist and others.
occult	relating to ghosts and the supernatural.
partition	the division of Ireland.
poverty	being very poor.
reprieved	given a less harsh punishment than originally decided on, or had a punishment cancelled or postponed.
séances	meetings where people try to contact the dead.
senate	in Ireland this is the part of the parliament that discusses new laws.
socialism	the belief that a country's wealth should be owned by everyone and not just by a small group of the very rich.
soup kitchens	places where free soup is given to hungry people.
state funeral	a funeral where the government organises a special ceremony.

strike	when a group of employees refuse to work because of a dispute with their employers over wages or working conditions.
submit	to accept or give in to something.
surrendered	gave up their weapons and stopped fighting.
taoiseach	the leader of the Irish government, like the prime minister in Britain.
trade unions	groups organised by workers to protect their rights and to discuss pay and working conditions with their employers.
UDA	Ulster Defence Association – an unofficial military group dedicated to keeping Northern Ireland as part of Britain.
United Nations Commissioner for Human Rights	the person given the job by the United Nations of helping people whose government tries to take away their right to say what they think, or to a fair trial if they are arrested, or to be treated well if they are in prison.
victorious	having won a battle.
Vikings	people who lived in Sweden or Denmark in the eighth to the eleventh centuries, and who raided the countries south of them by boat.

For teachers and parents

This book looks at famous Irish men and women within the five main historical eras. It is designed to develop children's knowledge, understanding and skills in History. To develop awareness of chronology, the people are presented in chronological order. Throughout the book and in the associated activities children are encouraged to use a range of historical skills and to understand how the characteristic features of a period impact on the people involved. There are opportunities for children to make links between situations and to identify changes across different periods. Children are also encouraged to see that the people's achievements were long-term, influencing many generations in many countries.

Whilst providing guidance, the activities are designed as starting points for further research, and in every case the children should plan their work carefully, select from the information available in this book and elsewhere, and present their findings appropriately. The activities are designed principally to develop history skills, but often make links with other curriculum subjects. Children should use ICT where appropriate, particularly for research and presentation. However, they should be encouraged to make sensible judgements about the accuracy of information drawn from the Internet.

SUGGESTED FURTHER ACTIVITIES

Pages 6–7 Brian Bórú

Children could use the Internet to research more details of Brian's conquest of Ireland. They could check this against the map on page 6 and add any areas that are not included with their dates of conquest.

Why was Sitric Silkenbeard given that name? Children could make up a Viking-style name for themselves and their friends. This might provide an opportunity for explaining alliteration.

Pages 8–9 Grace O'Malley

Children could investigate the story behind Grace's nickname, Gráinne Mhaol (Gráinne is the Irish for Grace, and Maol for bald). The story goes that she chopped off her hair so that her father would allow her to sail on his ships. Children could answer a series of questions such as why would she cut off her hair? What other things might she have to do to be a pirate? Wear trousers? Use a sword? Fight in battles?

Children could find out what ships were like in Grace O'Malley's time and draw pictures of Granuaile and her pirate ships.

Pages 10–11 W. B. Yeats

Children could search for other Irish Nobel Prize-winners at http://www.nobelprizes.com/

They could make a list of other famous Irish writers and find out more about them. These could include Bram Stoker, Jonathan Swift, Samuel Becket, Oscar Wilde, George Bernard Shaw, James Joyce, Roddy Doyle, John McGahern.

Children could make an illustrated timeline of famous Irish writers and see if there was a period when lots of people were successful as writers. Which ones have students heard about before (*Gulliver's Travels, Dracula*)?

Pages 12–13 James Connolly

Children can find out more about James Connolly's political beliefs at http://www.historylearningsite.co.uk/james_connolly.htm.

Teachers could start a classroom discussion on how fair it was for British landlords to charge rent on farms that they never visited or improved when Irish people were so poor. Half the class could represent the landlords and the other half could represent the people who worked hard on the farms to meet the rent.

Children could find out more about the 1913 Lock-Out at http://www.larkspirit.com/history/easter.html. They could decide who was right and who was wrong. They could consider what would be the result today if employers refused to let their employees back to work unless they agreed to accept worse conditions, such as a pay cut or longer hours.

They could find more information on the Easter Rising, including photos of the damage, lists of those executed and what the British and American newspapers said.
• http://www.nli.ie has archive photos and maps.
• http://www.bbc.co.uk/history/british/easterrising has sound archives as well as photographs.

Page 14–15 Constance Markievicz

There are many photographs of Constance showing her as a beauty, riding her horse or dressed in fashionable clothes, and also showing her dressed as a soldier. Children could investigate the different sides to her character through photographs. The following websites have photographs and biographies:
• http://www.thewildgeese.com/pages/ireland.html
• http://www.constancemarkievicz.ie/exhibition.php
• http://www.historylearningsite.co.uk/countess_markievicz.htm

Teachers could explain the issues surrounding the Anglo-Irish Treaty and partition, taking the oath of allegiance to the crown, accepting the treaty as a temporary measure, the role of religion etc. Children can decide whether they would have supported the treaty or not. See *War and Change: Ireland 1918–1924* in the Step-Up History series for more activities relating to this topic.

Pages 16–17 James Joyce

At http://www.online-literature.com/james_joyce/ or www.readprint.com/author-52/James-Joyce children can find out more about James Joyce's life. The sites also contain online editions of *Dubliners* and *Ulysses* and his poetry. Teachers might like to extract some of this and read it with students. Be aware of the explicit and difficult nature of some of the material.

Children could have a classroom discussion about why Joyce left Ireland when he did, and why he hardly ever returned to the country of his birth.

Joyce was alive right through the Easter Rising, the war with Britain and the civil war. His contemporary Yeats got involved in the new state. Children could compare the lives and characters of these two literary figures and suggest reasons for their attitudes towards the political situation in Ireland at the time.

Children could research Joyce's other works – *Dubliners*, *A Portrait of the Artist as a Young Man*, *Finnegan's Wake*. They could try reading a sentence or two from *Finnegan's Wake* and write a story of their own using their own made-up language.

Pages 18–19 Éamon de Valera and Michael Collins

Children could watch two films – *The Wind that Shakes the Barley* and *Michael Collins* – which put the two sides of the argument well. They could discuss in more detail the pros and cons of the Treaty and go on to compare the Neil Jordan film with a more objective account of Collins' life and the events of 1916–22.

Children might consider what could have happened if Collins had not been assassinated. Would the two men have found a way to cooperate after the war? Would Collins' popularity have meant that de Valera was never taoiseach? Would Collins, an able soldier and tactician, have been good as an ordinary politician?

Pages 20–21 Gerry Adams and Ian Paisley

Children could investigate and discuss some of the issues that surround Northern Ireland. These might include internment during the Troubles, using the army against British citizens, the media ban on Gerry Adams, whether it is justifiable to take up arms against a government, and what right Britain has to rule part of another country.

Pages 22–23 Mary Robinson

Children might consider what it would be like to live in a country where people could not get divorced. They could write a list of all the good and bad points of a law banning it.

The Elders are funded by an independent group of rich people such as Richard Branson. What would it be like if they were funded by, say, the American government or the Chinese government?

Children could find out more about the causes Mary Robinson has taken up and suggest some ways of solving those problems.

Pages 24–25 Bono

There is some controversy over celebrities' involvement in charity. Children could have a classroom discussion on whether they think charity and aid is really helpful or just makes rich westerners feel better.

Charity work is not only something that wealthy people like Bono can contribute to. Children could look at some of the issues supported by celebrities and discuss the ways ordinary people could support them, without having a lot of money – buying Fair Trade goods, for example.

Children could find out about the other members of U2 and where Bono and The Edge got their unusual names. They could look up their birthplaces on a map or create a timeline of the history of the band.

Pages 26–27 Roy Keane and Sonia O'Sullivan

Children could investigate the relationship between Manchester United and Irish players. Many of them came from Ireland. They can find out how much the team's Irish players have contributed.

Students can discuss the relationship between an athlete and their manager. Was Keane wrong to make such a public fuss and possibly cause Ireland to be knocked out of the competition? Should McCarthy have handled a clearly temperamental player better? Did Keane have a case to argue?

For both of these athletes students can talk about the differences between effort and outcome – Keane's huge income and O'Sullivan's much lower one. They could find out what the training regime for each of them is or was, and discuss whether it is better to be a footballer with all the injuries and newspaper interest and a huge paycheck, or a runner with a lower income and less press interest.

BOOKS

Seán Duffy (Ed.), *Atlas of Irish History* (Gill & Macmillan, 1997)

R. F. Foster (Ed.), *Oxford Illustrated History of Ireland* (OUP, 1989)

Brian Lalor (Ed.), *Encyclopaedia of Ireland* (Gill & Macmillan, 2003)

Christopher Wright, *A Children's History of Britain and Ireland* (Kingfisher Books, 1993)

Aubrey Flegg, *Katie's War: a story of the Irish Civil War* (O'Brien Press, 1997)

Index